Good Morning to You, Valentine

poems selected by
Lee Bennett Hopkins

illustrated by
Tomie de Paola

Harcourt Brace Jovanovich
New York and London

also edited by Lee Bennett Hopkins

HEY-HOW FOR HALLOWEEN!

SING HEY FOR CHRISTMAS DAY!

Printed in the United States of America

B C D E F G H I J K

LEE BENNETT HOPKINS for "Valentine Feelings," Copyright © 1975 by Lee Bennett Hopkins.

HUMPTY DUMPTY'S MAGAZINE for "If I Were a Mailman" by Vivian Gouled, copyright © by Parents' Magazine Enterprises, Inc., 1970.

ALFRED A. KNOPF, INC., for "February" by John Updike from *A Child's Calendar* by John Updike, illustrated by Nancy Ekholm Burkert. Copyright © 1965 by John Updike and Nancy Burkert.

McGRAW-HILL BOOK COMPANY for "Valentine for Earth" by Frances Frost from *The Little Naturalist* by Frances Frost and illustrated by Kurt Werth. Copyright © 1959 by the Estate of Frances Frost and Kurt Werth.

RAYMOND RICHARD PATTERSON for "A Love Song."

MELVIN LEE STEADMAN, JR., for "A Sure Sign" by Nancy Byrd Turner.

Library of Congress Cataloging in Publication Data
Main entry under title:

Good morning to you, Valentine.

SUMMARY: An anthology of twenty-three Valentine poems.
1. St. Valentine's Day—Juvenile poetry. [1. St. Valentine's Day—Poetry]
I. Hopkins, Lee Bennett.
PZ8.3.G6 821'.08 75-11650
ISBN 0-15-232134-9

To Barbara Lucas
—with so much love!

GOOD MORNING

Good morning to you, Valentine;
Curl your locks as I do mine,
One before and two behind,
Good morning to you, Valentine.

Anonymous

FEBRUARY

The sun rides higher
  Every trip.
The sidewalk shows.
  Icicles drip.

A snowstorm comes,
  And cars are stuck,
And ashes fly
  From the old town truck.

The chickadees
  Grow plump on seed
That Mother pours
  Where they can feed,

And snipping, snipping
  Scissors run
To cut out hearts
  For everyone.

John Updike

SOMEBODY

Somebody loves you deep and true.
If I weren't so bashful, I'd tell you who.

Anonymous

Tomorrow is Saint Valentine's day,
  All in the morning betime,
And I a maid at your window
  To be your Valentine.

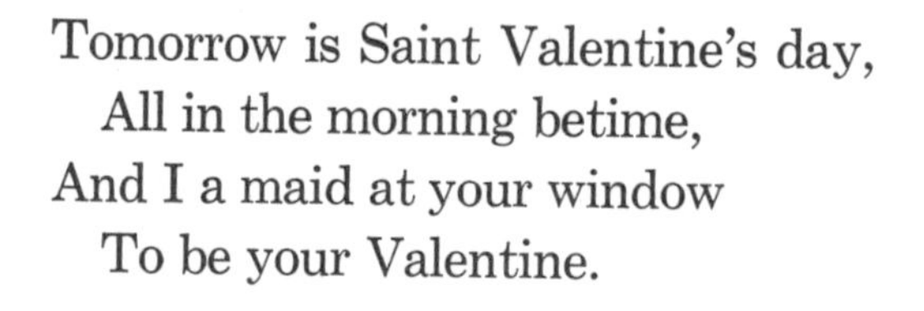

William Shakespeare

VALENTINE'S DAY
A cupid, a heart, and a dove,
And a sweet little message of love–
Oh, that's what I got
For the one who a lot
Of this day I have spent thinking *ove*.
Anonymous

OH, GOLDEN HEART

Oh, Golden Heart,
Be on your way.
Go, speed along
To sweetly say
That on this good
St. Valentine's Day
A heart is meant
To give away.

Anonymous

IF I WERE A MAILMAN

If I were a mailman,
   Know what I'd do?
I'd always bring mail
   With letters for YOU!

And on Valentine's Day
   I'd bring you plenty.
I might even bring you
   THREE HUNDRED AND TWENTY!

Vivian Gouled

A SURE SIGN

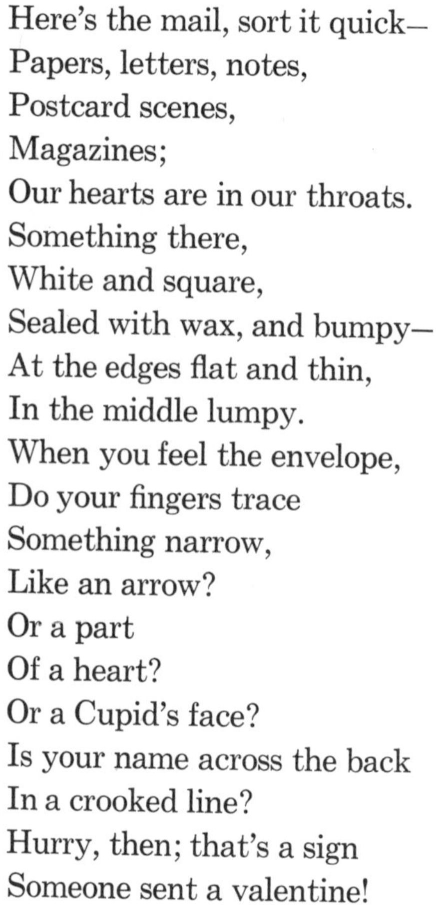

Here's the mail, sort it quick—
Papers, letters, notes,
Postcard scenes,
Magazines;
Our hearts are in our throats.
Something there,
White and square,
Sealed with wax, and bumpy—
At the edges flat and thin,
In the middle lumpy.
When you feel the envelope,
Do your fingers trace
Something narrow,
Like an arrow?
Or a part
Of a heart?
Or a Cupid's face?
Is your name across the back
In a crooked line?
Hurry, then; that's a sign
Someone sent a valentine!

Nancy Byrd Turner

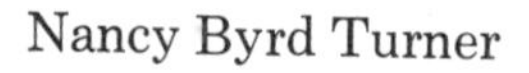

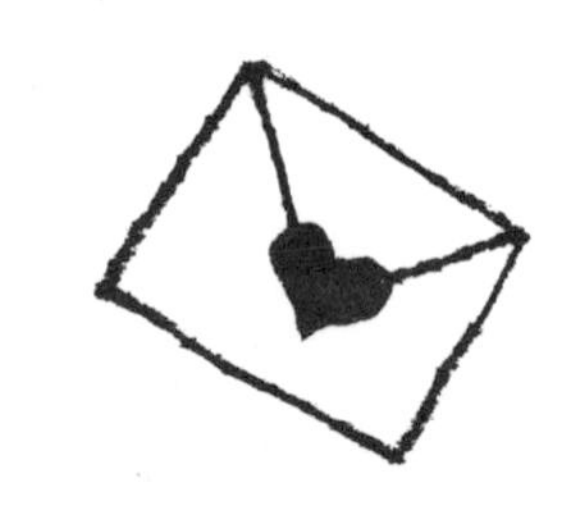

BE
MINE

VALENTINE FEELINGS

I feel flippy,
I feel fizzy,
I feel whoopy,
I feel whizzy.

I'm feeling wonderful.
I'm feeling just fine.
Because you just gave me
A valentine.

Lee Bennett Hopkins

ME 4 U

Roses are red
Violets are blue,
R U 4 me?
I am 4 U!

Anonymous

READ SEE THAT ME

Read see that me
up will I love
and you love you
down and you and

Anonymous

I LOVE YOU

I love you, I love you,
I love you divine,
Please give me your bubble gum,
You're *sitting* on mine!

Anonymous

TO MY VALENTINE

If apples were pears,
And peaches were plums,
And the rose had a different name;
If tigers were bears,
And fingers were thumbs,
I'd love you just the same!

Anonymous

CONVERSATION HEARTS

In February, bring them home,
pink, yellow, lavender
and lime pastels
BE MINE I'M YOURS
to be read by the tongue
that licks the chalk
and tastes what it spells.

I'll give you a boxful,
tasting of daphne, lupin,
mint and columbine;
a mouthful of secrets,
lovelier than whispers,
dear ones, friends
I'M YOURS BE MINE

Nina Payne

SNOWMAN'S VALENTINE

Faye made a snowman, fat and fine,
And, oh, how his button eyes did shine
　　When little Faye
　　Gave him today
A big red heart for a valentine.

Kay Dee

VALENTINES

I gave a hundred Valentines.
A hundred, did I say?
I gave a *thousand* Valentines
one cold and wintry day.

I didn't put my name on them
or any other words,
because my Valentines were seeds
for February birds.

Aileen Fisher

VALENTINE FROM A BIRD

Swinging high, high, high in the maple tree
Was the prettiest bird I ever did see,
    Chirping, "I love you,
    I do-do-do"–
A valentine love song–and all for me!

Anonymous

VALENTINE FOR EARTH

Oh, it will be fine
To rocket through space
And see the reverse
Of the moon's dark face,

To travel to Saturn
Or Venus or Mars,
Or maybe discover
Some uncharted stars.

But do they have anything
Better than we?
Do you think, for instance,
They have a blue sea

For sailing and swimming?
Do the planets have hills
With raspberry thickets
Where a song sparrow fills

The summer with music?
And do they have snow
To silver the roads
Where the school buses go?

Oh, I'm all for rockets
And worlds cold or hot,
But I'm wild in love
With the planet we've got.

Frances Frost

THE BEST VALENTINE

Some valentines are paper,
Shaped like hearts of pink and gold.
Some valentines are flowers
In a soft green tissue fold.
Some valentines are candy,
But the one I got instead
Was a furry little puppy
With a collar that was red.

Margaret Hillert

A LOVE SONG

Do I love you?
I'll tell you true.

Do chickens have lips?
Do pythons have hips?

Do penguins have arms?
Do spiders have charms?

Do oysters get colds?
Do leopards have moles?

Does a bird cage make a zoo?
Do I love you?

Raymond Richard Patterson

QUESTION

Do you love me
Or do you not?
You told me once
But I forgot.

Anonymous

THE JETS LUV FLORA

J.B. + M.P.

VALENTINE

I got a valentine from Timmy
Jimmy
Tillie
Billie
Nicky
Micky
Ricky
Dicky
Laura
Nora
Cora
Flora
Donnie
Ronnie
Lonnie
Connie
Eva even sent me two
But I didn't get *none* from you.

Shel Silverstein

MIX-UP

I climbed up the door
And shut the stairs
I said my shoes
And took off my prayers.

I shut off the bed
And climbed into the light
And all because–
She kissed me Goodnight.

Anonymous

INDEX